KID SCIENTIST
Zoologists on the Trail

Sue Fliess
illustrated by Mia Powell

Albert Whitman & Company
Chicago, Illinois

For Chris and Lorna—SF

Thank you to my wonderful Tom and Elvis—MP

Library of Congress Cataloging-in-Publication data
is on file with the publisher.

Text copyright © 2024 by Sue Fliess
Illustrations copyright © 2024 by Albert Whitman & Company
Illustrations by Mia Powell
First published in the United States of America
in 2024 by Albert Whitman & Company
ISBN 978-0-8075-4138-8 (hardcover)
ISBN 978-0-8075-4139-5 (ebook)

Printed in China
10 9 8 7 6 5 4 3 2 1 WKT 28 27 26 25 24 23

Design by Rick DeMonico

For more information about Albert Whitman & Company,
visit our website at www.albertwhitman.com.

"*Arooooooooo*," cries Kai.

"You've been practicing," says Yui.

"Your howl sounds real!" says Ravi.

Wyatt adds, "The wolves might consider you one of the pack now."

Kai, Yui, Wyatt, and Ravi are zoologists, or scientists who study animals and how they behave in their environments.

"I can't believe it's been a year since we've been here at Yellowstone National Park to check on the wolves," says Kai. The scientists return each spring to watch a pack of gray wolves.

Yui says, "I hope we learn that the wolves are still helping to restore the balance of the park's plants and animals."

"Yes, it would be good to see that the wolves are helping the park's ecosystem and staying healthy themselves," says Kai.
"Time to see how they're doing!" says Wyatt.

The team heads to the lab to meet up with a park ranger, who tells them that two of the wolves' radio collars have stopped working.

"That's too bad," says Kai. "Radio collars help us keep track of the wolves by sending signals to the antennae on the park's airplanes. The signals let us know where the wolves are, within twenty-five miles. Without the collars, it's hard to track, follow, and count the whole pack."

"Will we be replacing the broken collars?" asks Ravi.

"And adding collars to any new wolves?" asks Wyatt.

The team knows it's important to monitor the pack, but putting radio collars on animals comes with risks. When an animal gets a collar, it must be sedated, and sometimes it takes a while to wake up, leaving it vulnerable to weather and predators.

"Luckily, there are other ways to track them," says Kai.
"Instead of replacing the collars, I want to try a tracking
method called bioacoustics."

"Bio-who?" asks Yui.

Kai explains, "Bioacoustics is the study of making and receiving animal sounds. In my experiment, I'll use bioacoustics by howling to the wolves. If a wolf howls back, we'll record it."

"Wolves howl for lots of reasons," adds Wyatt. "To start a hunt, to find another wolf, to answer a pack's howls, or to warn that a territory is occupied."

"Each howl is unique," says Kai, "so we should be able to count and identify new wolves. The pack has been growing each year and the park is thriving. My hypothesis, or educated guess, is that the wolf pack will have grown this year, too."

"I'll help test Kai's hypothesis by checking the pack's health and diet," says Yui. "Only a healthy pack can grow, so I'll collect and examine their scat, or poop, for signs they're eating well."

"And Ravi and I will observe and document changes to the park's ecosystem since the first pack of wolves was reintroduced in the 1990s," says Wyatt. "We'll take photos with our cameras and drones and compare them with images taken before the wolves returned."

The ranger points out places on the map where the wolves have been spotted. The scientists head to each location with their equipment to check for signs of the pack.

"Here!" says Yui. "I found wolf tracks and scat." She collects the scat, places it in a bag, and labels the bag with the date and location. "I can tell this scat is fresh because it is wet and black, which means wolves were here only an hour or two ago. I'll examine it later at the lab." She takes photos and measures the tracks.

Just then, Ravi shouts, "Team, come quickly!" Everyone hurries over to see that Ravi has found a wolf den. "This large pile of dirt in front of the burrow was my clue," she says. "It marks the den's entrance."

"Jackpot," says Kai.

Wyatt and Ravi set up motion-sensor cameras to capture video of the wolves. "Hopefully these will help us count the number of wolves in the pack and observe their behavior," says Wyatt.

Ravi also flies a drone to take video and photos of the landscape.

As they are leaving, they hear a yelp coming from the den. Ravi crouches and sees a wolf cub peeking out of the entrance. Ravi takes a picture and whispers, "Let's go before any more wake up. We don't want to disturb them."

"We'll return to this area tonight because wolves are most active at dawn and dusk," says Kai.

That evening, the team heads back into wolf territory.

Kai goes over the plan. "I'll get out of the car at different points to howl, and Ravi will record any wolf responses with a microphone."

"Hopefully, they'll howl back," says Wyatt.

"I'm depending on it!" says Kai.

Soon, Kai gets out of the car and howls, "*Aroooooooooo!*" The scientists listen but don't hear anything. Kai takes a few steps down the trail and howls again.

A wolf howls back. "*Awooeeeoooo!*" The team moves closer to the sound, and Kai repeats the process. More wolves respond with their unique howls. "*Aaaaaariiioooooo!*"

"This is amazing!" says Yui.

"It's like we're part of the pack," adds Wyatt.

"I think I counted at least five different howls," says Ravi.

"Maybe more," says Kai. "To learn the correct number, we'll listen to them again in the lab and compare the howls."

FRUIT
SEED

SCAT

ELK
HAIR

LEAF

After two weeks of gathering and analyzing data to be sure they have enough samples for accurate conclusions, the team reviews everything they've found.

"I'm happy to announce these scat samples are definitely from a healthy pack of wolves!" says Yui. "I found fruit seeds, leaf fragments, and deer and elk hair. Only a group of healthy wolves working together can successfully hunt prey that large."

"And Ravi and I compared our park photos to the ones taken before the wolves were reintroduced," says Wyatt. "We found the landscape has changed—for the better! Years ago, when there were too many deer, they ate all the vegetation. But the wolves are keeping the deer population down, so plants, berries, and even insects have come back.

Ravi adds, "Our motion-sensor cameras show the pack walking around, strong and healthy. And our drone footage shows that other animals have moved back to the park too."

"After studying our videos and listening to the howl recordings," says Kai, "I'm excited to report that I identified our original seven wolves...plus four new members of the pack!"

The team cheers.

Kai continues, "This confirms my hypothesis that the pack is healthy and growing. But, maybe more importantly, our study supports the fact that reintroducing wolves to Yellowstone helped restore the park's ecosystem."

"I can't believe it's time to *pack* up again," says Kai, and everyone groans.

"Until next year!" says Yui.

WHAT IS A ZOOLOGIST?

Zoologists are scientists who study and classify animals and how they interact with their environment. Zoologists learn how animals live, move, and eat, and how they behave in groups or by themselves.

These scientists also work closely with wild animals in laboratories, zoos, and natural habitats such as deserts, grasslands, and rain forests. Zoologists who study wolves, like the scientists in this book, are also called wildlife biologists.

All scientists conduct research by following the steps of the scientific method. Kai and his team used each step to guide their research.

STEPS OF THE SCIENTIFIC METHOD

1. Make observations and do background research. Kai and his team wanted to track wolves to see if they were thriving. They compared earlier observations and data with what they found on this trip. They researched what makes a healthy wolf, as well as methods of tracking wolves.

2. Ask questions about your observations and gather information. Knowing some of the wolves' tracking collars had stopped working, they asked what other ways they could observe the pack to see if it was healthy and growing.

3. Form a hypothesis. After learning that several of the collars had stopped working, Kai used bioacoustics to track the wolf population and identify new wolves. His hypothesis was that the pack is growing.

4. Perform an experiment and collect data. Kai howled to the wolves, and Ravi recorded their answering howls to identify individual wolves and see if their pack number had grown. Wyatt and Ravi gathered information about the park, its ecosystems, and how the landscape had changed since the wolves were reintroduced. Yui gathered wolf scat to determine the health of the pack and learn more about their diet.

5. Analyze the data and draw conclusions. Consider how the conclusions support or disprove your hypothesis. Once the team reviewed their findings, they were able to conclude that not only was the pack healthy and growing; it had changed the park's ecosystem for the better. Their findings confirmed each team members' hypotheses.

6. Communicate or present your findings. After gathering their data, Kai and his team will publish their research supporting the hypothesis that the wolf pack is healthy, growing, and improving the park's ecosystem, and how they arrived at that conclusion.

HOW CAN I BECOME A ZOOLOGIST?

Zoologists want to spend time with animals and learn all about them. But there are many ways to study animals, even before you decide on a career.

- Check out books or videos at your local library.

- Visit a nearby zoo or wildlife park to observe animals. It's also a great opportunity to ask questions of zoologists who work there.

- Observe animals close to home in a park or garden. Bird-watching is a good way to learn about animals and their environments.

- When you're outside, try to identify bird and animal calls, insects you see, and even scat you might find.

When you're older, you can attend a college that offers a science degree and choose to study zoology. When you are a zoologist, your research or conservation work could help save endangered species. As a zoologist or wildlife biologist, you will do fieldwork, conduct research, collect data, and write reports. You might even manage a wildlife park!

SUGGESTED READING FOR KIDS

Barr, Catherine. *The Wolves of Yellowstone: A Rewilding Story*. New York: Bloomsbury Children's Books, 2022.

Isabella, Jude, and Kim Smith. *Bringing Back the Wolves : How a Predator Restored an Ecosystem*. Toronto: Kids Can Press, 2020.

Patent, Dorothy Hinshaw. *When the Wolves Returned: Restoring Nature's Balance in Yellowstone*. New York: Walker, 2008.